Table of Contents

Introduction

Breakfast Recipes

    French Breakfast Crepe

    Pain au Chocolat (Chocolate Croissants)

    French Omelet

    Eggs and Black Truffles

    Quiche Lorraine

    French Toast with Grand Marnier

    Stuffed Breakfast Baguette

    Brioche with Poached Eggs and Pistou

    French Baguette

Beef/Veal Dishes

    Boeuf en Croute (Beef in a Pastry Shell)

    Steak Diane

    Boeuf Bourguignon

    Steak au Poivre (Pepper Steak)

    Hachis Parmentier

Chicken Recipes

    Poulet à la Crème (Chicken in Cream Sauce)

    Chicken Cordon Bleu Recipe

    Poulet Basquaise – Chicken and Tomato Casserole

    Roasted Chicken with Garlic

    Coq au Vin

Duck Recipes

    Duck Cassoulet

    Canard a l'Orange (Duck with Orange Sauce)

    (Canard aux Framboises) Duck Breasts with Raspberry Sauce

Pork Recipes

    Croque Madame and Croque Monsieur

    Pork Aux Champignons (Pork and Mushrooms)

    Pork in Port Wine

- Lamb Recipes
  - Lamb Navarin
  - Roast Leg of Lamb
  - Gigot a La Cuillère (Slow Simmered Lamb)
- Seafood Recipes
  - Trout Meunière Amandine (Trout with Brown Butter Sauce and Almonds)
  - Moules à la Marinière
  - Salmon Crepes
  - Cognac Shrimp
  - Bouillabaisse
- Lighter French Fare (Soup and Salads)
  - Asparagus and Ham with Poached Egg
  - Macaroni Beaucaire
  - Salade au Chèvre Chaud (Goat Cheese Salad)
  - Salad Niçoise
  - Onion Tart
  - (Tartiflette) (Bacon, Potato, and Reblochon Casserole)
  - Soupe a l'oignon (French Onion Soup)
  - Potage Parmentier (Potato and Leek Soup)
  - Cauliflower and Cheese Soufflé
  - Ratatouille
  - Pan Bagnat
- Desserts
  - Chocolate Banana Crepes
  - Cappuccino Soufflé
  - Pots de Créme
  - Crêpes Suzette
  - Peach Melba
  - Baked Brie
  - Creme Brulee
- Author's Afterthoughts

Introduction

Many of us associate French cooking with haute cuisine – snobby food by served even snobbier waiters. The truth is, French cooking is founded on cuisine du potager and cuisine du marché - food from the garden and food from the market. The poor ate whatever food was close-by. French recipes rarely have complicated ingredients that can't be grown locally. A French diet consists of fresh food that is cooked simply, but well. The French have also taken advantage of their proximity to the sea to use fresh fish in many delicious ways. Possibly, no other country is as renowned for its delectable seafood fare as the French. This cookbook contains a number of tasty examples.

Another thing that differentiates French cooking from many others is their love of butter. Butter makes any recipe taste better, and it's an important part of French cuisine. Interestingly, most French are slim, without showing any hint of such indulgence. Their secret? Just as they eat naturally, they move naturally. The French walk and cycle instead of driving. They take the stairs instead of the escalator. Butter doesn't stand a chance.

It's the French love of food that has elevated simple cuisine into haute. French chefs, such as Larousse and Escoffier, have promoted French cooking techniques to the world. And let's not forget Julia Child and Jacque Pepin ... Their techniques can raise the level of your cooking as much as good, fresh ingredients. Let's take a look at some of these very French ways of preparing food:

Sautéing is a popular method of food preparation. It uses less fat than frying and still cooks food quickly.

Poaching prepares food placed in boiling water or milk and simmers food without losing any of the flavor. While poaching is mostly associated with eggs, fish and chicken can also be poached.

Braising meat imparts extra flavor from the braising liquid. Since braising is a slow way to prepare food, it works well with cheap meats that benefit from the extra cooking time.

Flambéing desserts or meats provides a lot of heat and leaves the delicious flavor of the alcohol that was used to flambé.

Of course, what is French cooking without wine? Wine and other spirits add more layers of complexity and flavor to any ingredient, and they keep the food moist. France is famous for its wines, and it's a natural step to use locally produced wines in food preparation. Alcohol will quickly dissipate during cooking, so you don't have to worry about contributing to any bad habits. When using wines and other liqueurs, use the kind of spirits you would actually drink. Never use anything labelled "cooking wine." The French will get quite upset with you. For them, good food and good wine go together naturally. So, serve whatever wine you used for cooking to fill a glass at the table. A votre Sante! The French toast to your health is a reminder that despite its reputation, French cooking is actually quite healthy and simple.

Breakfast Recipes

French Breakfast Crepe

Crepes are versatile enough for you to prepare for breakfast, dinner or dessert. It's all about the filling. The French love them so much, they've given the crepe its own holiday. February 2 is known as "jour des crêpes," or Day of Crepes. Traditionally, on that day, you hold a crepe pan in one hand and a coin in another. The crepe gets tossed into the air. If you catch it back into the pan, you'll enjoy a year of prosperity. And you'll get the enjoy the crepe, as well. Using a cast-iron skillet will make a huge difference in how your crepe turns out.

Servings: 6

Cooking Time: 12

Ingredients:

- 1 ½ cups milk
- 3 large eggs
- 4 tbsp. sugar
- 1 teaspoon salt
- 5 Tbsp. unsalted butter
- 3 Tbsp. brandy
- 1 tsp. vanilla
- 1 cup white flour
- Extra butter for preparing crepes

Directions:

1. Use a blender or a bowl to whip the eggs and milk. A blender is better.
2. Add the salt and sugar and continue blending.
3. Melt the butter in a small saucepan.
4. Stir the melted butter, vanilla, and brandy into the batter.
5. Mix in the flour and blend until the batter is smooth.
6. Heat up your skillet on high.
7. Melt just a bit of the extra butter in the skillet. It should get to the point of almost smoking
8. Still at high heat, cook the crepe for a minute or so. Check the crepe by lifting the edges. You don't want them burned.
9. When one side is nice and brown, flip the crepe over and cook for another minute or so.
10. Keep the crepe warm as you prepare the remaining batter.
11. To serve these French crepes, add a bit of apricot jam and fold them up.

Pain au Chocolat (Chocolate Croissants)

Fresh out of the oven, these beauties are a buttery, crispy, and flaky piece of heaven. Enjoy this luxurious treat with a cup of café au lait. The French relish them on Christmas morning.

Servings: 6

Cooking Time: 14 minutes

Ingredients:

- 4 tsp. dried yeast
- 3 ½ cups pastry flour
- ½ cup milk
- 1/3 cup sugar
- 4 Tbsp. melted butter
- 1 tsp. salt
- 1 cup softened butter
- 10 oz. chopped semisweet chocolate
- 1 egg
- 2 Tbsp. milk

Directions:

1. Mix the yeast into half a cup of warm water and let it dissolve.

2. Pour the dissolved yeast into a bowl and add the flour, sugar, milk, melted butter, and salt.

3. Use a hand mixer to incorporate the ingredients for 2 minutes.

4. If the mixture is sticky, add a bit more flour.

5. Form the dough into a ball and cover the bowl with a sheet of plastic.

6. Keep at room temperature for half an hour.

7. Place the dough on a flat surface and roll it into a 10 by 15 rectangle. Cover the rectangle with more plastic and let it sit for 40 minutes as the dough rises.

8. With a pastry brush, lightly cover the dough with the softened butter.

9. Fold the dough in three, like a letter. Cover it with plastic and refrigerate for an hour.

10. Cut the dough into 3 x 4 triangles.

11. Fill the short end of the triangle with 2 tsp. of chopped chocolate.

12. Fold the croissant up, starting with the short end.

13. Lightly butter a baking sheet.

14. Place the croissants on the sheet, leaving half an inch between each.

15. Again, cover the baking sheet with more plastic and let the dough rise for an hour.

16. Preheat the oven to 400 degrees F.

17. Whisk together 2 Tbsp. of milk and one egg for a wash.

18. Brush each croissant with the wash.

19. Bake for 14 minutes. They should be a nice, light brown.

French Omelet

Preparing the perfect omelet is in the technique. The French have elevated this simple dish with fresh herbs to create a savory delicacy. Use the freshest eggs you can find.

Serves: 2

Cooking Time: 20 minutes

Ingredients:

- 10 large fresh eggs
- Salt and pepper to taste
- 1/3 cup parsley
- 5 Tbsp. chives
- 5 Tbsp. chervil
- 3 Tbsp. butter

Directions:

1. Whip the eggs in a bowl and add the herbs.
2. Heat the butter in a skillet. Pour in half of the beaten eggs.
3. Stir and keep shaking the pan.
4. When the eggs start to become solid, stop stirring. Let cook for 8 to 10 minutes.

5. Fold the omelet in half and slide onto a plate.
6. Use the remaining eggs to make a second omelet.

Eggs and Black Truffles

Serves: 4

Cooking Time: 10 minutes

These eggs are velvety smooth. The truffles add a special decadence that makes this French egg dish perfect for a special occasion or weekend treat.

Ingredients:

- 8 large eggs
- 1 oz. shaved black truffles
- 6 Tbsp. softened butter
- Salt and pepper to taste

Directions:

1. Use a double boiler and bring water to the simmering point in the bottom portion.
2. In the top part, whisk the eggs, butter, and shaved truffles.
3. Don't stop whisking those eggs. They should look like cottage cheese.
4. Transfer the eggs to a plate and season with the salt and pepper.

Quiche Lorraine

Quiche Lorraine originated during the middle ages, when Lorraine was still under German rule. But the Germans aren't getting any credit for this. This has long been a French classic. A quiche is a custard pie that can be filled any favorite ingredients. The Quiche Lorraine is made with savory bacon. Who could resist? A type of quiche was served at the coronation of King Henry IV in 1399. But he didn't get any bacon. (Maybe because he wasn't French.)

Servings: 6

Cooking Time: 45 minutes

Ingredients:

- 4 slices of bacon
- 1 frozen pastry shell
- 3 large eggs
- 1 ½ cups heavy cream
- Pinches of salt, pepper and nutmeg
- 2 Tbsp. of cut-up butter

Directions:

1. Preheat the oven to 375 degrees F.

2. Chop the bacon into 1-inch pieces. Simmer the bacon in 4 cups of water for 5 minutes. This was Julia Child's way of cutting down on the smoky

flavor.

3. Dry the bacon pieces on a paper towel.

4. Brown the bacon in a skillet and lay the pieces on the bottom of the pie shell.

5. Whip the eggs, heavy cream, salt, pepper and nutmeg in a bowl.

6. Pour the eggs on top of the bacon.

7. Place the cut-up butter pieces on top.

8. Bake for about 40 minutes. The quiche should be nicely browned.

French Toast with Grand Marnier

Does it seem that the people of France put a lot of liquor in their breakfasts? It's something to ponder. You can use orange juice instead, but where's the fun in that? This tasty dish is easy because it's started the night before. Sober or not, the French know how to treat an egg. The concept of French toast started when wives looked for ways to use stale bread. Using day-old bread still makes the best French toast.

Serves: 6

Cooking Time: 35 minutes

Ingredients:

- 4 large eggs
- 4 cups whipping cream
- 4 Tbsp. Grand Marnier or orange juice
- 4 Tbsp. sugar
- 1 Tbsp. orange zest
- 1 loaf of French bread

Directions:

1. Cut the bread into 12 slices and place them in a baking dish.
2. Mix the remaining ingredients well and pour over the bread.

3. Refrigerate the dish overnight.

4. In the morning, preheat the oven to 375 degrees F.

5. Lightly butter a baking sheet.

6. Transfer the soaked bread slices to the baking sheet.

7. Bake for 35 minutes. Turn once during the baking.

8. Place the French toast on a platter and dust with confectioner's sugar. Serve with orange butter (see below).

Ingredients for Orange Butter:
- 6 oz. butter
- 4 Tbsp. orange juice
- 1 Tbsp. Grand Marnier
- 1/3 cup confectioner's sugar
- Zest from 1 orange

Directions:

1. Soften the butter by leaving it unrefrigerated.

2. Place the butter in a bowl and mix in all remaining ingredients and incorporate them well.

3. Refrigerate.

4. Before serving, microwave the orange butter and spoon over the French toast.

Stuffed Breakfast Baguette

Everyone loves crispy French bread. Stuffed with favorite breakfast goodies, it takes on a whole other dimension. This is perfect for a family breakfast.

Serves: 6

Cooking Time: 12 minutes

Ingredients:

- 1 package pork sausage
- 1 small chopped onion
- 1 cup chopped bell peppers
- ½ tsp. diced garlic
- ¼ cup melted butter
- 6 large eggs
- 2 Tbsp. milk or half & half
- 6 slices of sharp cheddar cheese
- 1 ½ cup shredded mozzarella

Directions:

1. Preheat the oven to 400 degrees F.
2. Line a baking sheet with foil or parchment paper.

3. Cook the sausage in a skillet and break it into small pieces.

4. Add in the garlic, onion, and bell pepper, and stir with a wooden spoon for about 5 minutes.

5. Cut the French baguette lengthwise.

6. Drizzle both baguette halves with half of the melted butter.

7. Cover with a piece of aluminum foil and place in the oven.

8. Bake for 10 to 12 minutes.

9. Whisk the eggs and the milk in a bowl.

10. Add the remaining melted butter to a skillet and scramble the eggs.

11. Remove the baguette from the oven and place on the counter.

12. Top the bread with slices of cheddar, the bell pepper mixture, the scrambled eggs, and the shredded mozzarella.

13. Return the bread to the oven and broil for a few minutes. The cheese should be melted, but watch that it doesn't burn.

14. If desired, sprinkle the bread with a bit of chopped chive.

15. Slice the baguette halves and serve warm

Brioche with Poached Eggs and Pistou

The French have taken Eggs Benedict and given it some needed therapy. Eggs Benedict suffers from a confused identity problem. With its French Hollandaise sauce, Canadian bacon and English muffin, it's hard to know what flag to fly. They've substituted a French brioche and a decidedly French herb mixture (pistou). These poached eggs can be paired with an Hermes scarf while singing the Marseillaise.

Serves: 2

Cooking Time: 3 minutes

Ingredients:

- 1/3 cup fresh basil
- 6 Tbsp. olive oil
- ½ garlic clove
- 4 eggs
- Brioche, sliced in half
- Grated Parmesan cheese

Directions:

1. Toast 2 brioche slices.

2. Place the basil, olive oil, and garlic in a food processor and puree to make the pistou.

3. Season the pistou with some salt and pepper.

4. Add 1 ½ inches of water to a skillet. Mix in some salt and bring the water to a slow simmer.

5. Crack the eggs and place carefully in the hot water.

6. Cook the eggs for 3 minutes; they'll be a bit runny.

7. Place the toasted brioche slices on a platter. Dust each with some parmesan.

8. Use a slotted spoon to transfer the poached eggs to the brioche, 2 eggs per slice.

9. Season the eggs with salt and pepper and drizzle with the pistou.

French Baguette

Many of the dishes in this book call for a baguette as part of the recipe or as an accompaniment. Preparing the baguette is very easy; it requires just a bit of kneading. A hot, crispy baguette is so tasty, you'll want to make it fresh whenever you have time in the morning.

Serves: 2 loaves

Cooking Time: 20

Ingredients:

- 2 ¼ tsp. of yeast
- 1 ¼ cup warm water
- 3 cups white flour
- ¾ tsp. salt
- 1 tsp. cornmeal

Directions:

1. Add the yeast to the warm water and let it dissolve.
2. Measure 2 ¾ cups of the flour and add to the yeast.
3. Keep stirring until the dough forms.
4. Cover with a cloth and let sit for 5 minutes.
5. Place the dough on a floured surface. Dust with the salt.
6. Knead for 5 – 6 minutes.
7. Add more flour to keep the dough from sticking.

8. Coat a bowl or platter with non-stick cooking spray and add the dough.

9. Cover with a cloth and let rise in a warm place for 40 minutes.

10. Punch the dough down and let rise for another 5 minutes.

11. Divide the dough in half and cover one half and work with the other.

12. Form the first half of the dough into a 12-inch oblong shape.

13. Repeat with the other half of the dough.

14. Place both pieces on a baking sheet and dust with the cornmeal.

15. Allow the dough to rise for another 12 minutes, while you preheat the oven to 450 degrees F.

16. Cut a few slashes across the dough.

17. Bake for 20 minutes.

Beef/Veal Dishes

Boeuf en Croute (Beef in a Pastry Shell)

This French beef dish is a piece of art worthy of Renoir. It's meant to impress and succeeds admirably. Since the beef is such a masterpiece, keep it in the spotlight with a simple side of asparagus or string beans.

Serves: 8

Cooking Time: 1 hour

Ingredients:

- 1 ½ cups sliced mushrooms
- 2 diced shallots
- 2 minced garlic cloves
- 4 tbsp. butter
- 1/2 cup Madeira wine
- 3 tbsp. heavy cream
- 1 tbsp. chopped parsley
- 2 lb. - beef tenderloin roast
- Salt and pepper to taste
- 1 tbsp. olive oil
- 2 frozen pastry sheets
- 1 egg

Directions:

1. Start by preparing the mushroom mixture. Sauté the mushrooms, garlic and shallots in the butter for 5 minutes.
2. Add the Madeira and stir until the wine mostly evaporates.
3. Add the heavy cream; stir until the sauce thickens, about 1 minute.
4. Add the chopped parsley and set the mushrooms aside.
5. Season the beef with the salt and pepper.
6. Heat up the olive oil and brown the meat until all sides are browned.
7. Preheat the oven to 425 degrees.
8. Cover a large baking sheet with parchment paper.
9. Place the pastry sheets on a floured counter and form a rectangle.
10. Spoon the mushrooms down the center.
11. Top the mushrooms with the beef tenderloin.
12. Wrap the sheets around the meat (like wrapping a present) pinching the seams together.
13. Cut off any excess pastry sheet.
14. Beat the egg and brush the entire pastry sheet -covered beef with the egg.
15. Place the meat on a baking sheet.
16. Adjust the oven temperature down to 400 degrees.
17. Roast the meat for 1 hour. This will produce rare meat. Roast a bit longer for more well-done. If the pastry browns too much too soon, cover it with some aluminum foil.
18. Let the roast sit before slicing. Serve with some roasted vegetables.

Steak Diane

Serves: 1

Cooking Time: 10 minutes

Steak Diane is named after the Goddess of the Hunt, Diana. The meat, preferably a good fillet mignon with a savory sauce, is set on fire tableside. French cooking at its most dramatic. It was famed French chef Auguste Escoffier who first made mention of the Steak a la Diana. The sauce is intense and luscious.

Ingredients:

- 2 good 8-oz. steak fillets
- Salt and pepper to taste
- 4 Tbsp. unsalted butter
- 5 Tbsp. minced shallots
- 2/3 cup sliced mushrooms
- 3 Tbsp. cognac
- 2/3 cup beef broth
- 2 tsp. Dijon mustard
- 2 tsp. Worcestershire sauce

Directions:

1. Pound the steaks until they are ¼ inch thick.
2. Season the fillets with the salt and pepper.
3. Melt 2 Tbsp. of the butter in a skillet. Cook the steaks 1 minute per side.
4. Transfer the steaks to a platter.
5. Reduce the heat and melt the remaining butter. Sauté the mushrooms and shallots until the shallots are translucent.
6. Turn up the heat and add the cognac. Stir. After half a minute, pour in half of the beef broth and scrape the bits on the bottom of the pan with a wooden spoon. These bits add a lot to the flavor.
7. Stir in the Worcestershire sauce and the mustard. Stir for about 2 minutes until the sauce reduces.
8. Transfer the steak fillets (with any juices) back into the pan. Flip them until they are coated with the mushroom sauce.
9. Cook the steaks to the doneness you prefer.
10. Light a wooden match or bamboo skewer and ignite the steaks.
11. Let the flame extinguish and remove the pan from the stove.
12. Check the seasoning and adjust.
13. Serve the steaks with the sauce.

Boeuf Bourguignon

Servings: 8

Cooking Time: 2 hours 50 minutes

This famous French stew comes from the Burgundy region, which is known for its fine and rich French cooking, as well as superb wines. Famed chef Auguste Escoffier put this dish on the map in 1903 and elevated it from a French peasant meal to haute cuisine. It is prepared by braising the beef in the region's full-bodied wine, along with vegetables and seasonings. Traditionally, this dish is simmered for 2 days, so it is an excellent dish to prepare in a slow cooker. The flavors really meld together on the second day.

Ingredients:

- 2 lbs. chuck or sirloin roast cut into bite-sized pieces
- Salt and pepper to taste
- ¼ cup olive oil
- 4 sliced onions
- 3 Tbsp. flour
- 1 cup burgundy wine
- 6 sliced carrots
- 1 minced garlic clove

- 1 bouquet garni (an herb bundle with bay leaves, parsley, and thyme)
- 1 cup beef broth or 2 Tbsp. demi-glace

Directions:

1. Heat the oil in a Dutch oven until it is very hot.
2. While the oil heats, season the beef cubes with salt and pepper.
3. Brown the meat in stages so as to avoid overcrowding. Make sure they are browned on all sides.
4. Once all the meat is browned, lower the heat.
5. Stir in the onions and cook for 10 minutes.
6. Cover the onions with the flour and stir with a wooden spoon. While stirring, remember to scrape the brown bits at the bottom of the Dutch oven.
7. Pour in the wine and bring to a boil.
8. Add the bouquet garni, garlic, and carrot to the pot.
9. Add water to cover the meat well. If you have any demi-glace, add 2 tablespoons. Or add a cup of beef broth.
10. Let the liquid boil, then lower the heat to a simmer for 2 to 2 and a half hours.
11. Check on the meat periodically to make sure it isn't sticking.
12. Remove the bouquet garni prior to serving.

Steak au Poivre (Pepper Steak)

Steak au Poivre is a good-quality steak, such as filet mignon, encrusted in peppercorn and served with a creamy sauce. It's a popular French bistro fare that pairs well with shoe-string potatoes.

Servings: 4

Cooking Time: 10 minutes

Ingredients:

- 4 6-oz. steaks that are about 1 ½" thick.
- Salt to taste
- 1 ½ Tbsp. peppercorns
- 2 Tbsp. butter
- 1/3 cup cognac
- 1 cup whipping cream

Directions:

1. Let the steaks rest at room temperature for an hour.

2. Season the steaks with salt.

3. Use a mallet or mortar and pestle to crush the peppercorns. Dust a plate with the crushed peppercorn.

4. Press both sides of the steaks into the crushed peppercorn.

5. Heat the butter in a skillet.

6. When the butter starts to bubble, sear the steaks on both sides, 4 minutes on each.

7. Place the steaks on a platter and cover with aluminum foil.

8. Raising the skillet above the heat, pour the cognac into the pan, and ignite it.

9. Shake the skillet until the flames are gone.

10. Place the skillet back on the stove and stir in the cream.

11. Let the liquid boil for about 5 minutes.

12. Put the steaks on their plates, and drizzle with the cream sauce.

13. Serve immediately.

Hachis Parmentier

Servings: 8

Cooking Time: 20 minutes

This is the French version of comfort food, and it's outstanding. It combines cheesy potatoes and braised beef to create French cooking perfection. In the late 18th century, French pharmacist Augustin Parmentier wanted to publicize the edibility of potatoes, which were not a very popular crop in France at the time, so he created this recipe. We should raise a glass of good French wine in his honor.

Ingredients:

- 2 chopped onions
- 3 minced garlic cloves
- 3 tablespoons olive oil
- 3 chopped tomatoes
- 2 lbs. ground beef
- 1 ¼ Tbsp. herbes de provence
- Salt and pepper to taste
- 1 egg yolk
- 3 Tbsp. grated parmesan cheese
- 5 cups mashed potatoes

- 3/4 – 1 cup gruyere cheese

Directions:

1. Heat the olive oil in a large skillet and sauté the onions and garlic for 5 minutes.
2. Add the ground beef, tomatoes, herbes de provence, salt, and pepper.
3. Cook until the beef turns brown.
4. Turn the oven off and stir in the egg yolk and grated parmesan cheese. Mix the ingredients thoroughly
5. Distribute the beef on the bottom of a baking dish.
6. Top the beef with the mashed potatoes.
7. Add the gruyere cheese on top of the potatoes.
8. Bake for 20 minutes at 400 degrees F.

Chicken Recipes

Poulet à la Crème (Chicken in Cream Sauce)

Cream sauce is a standard of French cooking. This Poulet a la Crème comes from Bourg-en-Bresse. The sauce is made of wine and heavy cream and is easy to prepare. A dash of tarragon gives it a nice kick. Serve it with a side of rice.

Serves 4

Cooking Time: 30 minutes

Ingredients:

- 2 Tbsp. butter
- 2 ½ lbs. chicken thighs without skin
- ½ cup sliced mushrooms
- 1 ½ Tbsp. flour
- ½ cup white wine
- ¼ cup water
- Salt and pepper to taste
- ½ cup whipping cream
- 1 Tbsp. chopped tarragon

Directions:

1. In a large skillet, brown the chicken in the melted butter until each side is nicely browned.

2. Add in mushrooms and dust the chicken and mushrooms with the flour.
3. Pour in the water and wine and stir.
4. Let the liquid boil and add the seasoning.
5. Lower the heat and cover the pan.
6. Simmer for 25 to 30 minutes, until the chicken is done.
7. Stir in the whipping cream and bring the sauce to a boil for a minute.
8. Add the tarragon and serve.

Chicken Cordon Bleu Recipe

Chicken Cordon Bleu is an elegant dish that is easy to prepare. The chicken remains incredibly juicy. The ham and cheese just melt in your mouth. A little secret from French chefs? Make a little extra sauce and use it as gravy over mashed potatoes. Tres bon!

Servings: 6

Cooking Time: 30 minutes

Ingredients:

- 6 skinless and boneless chicken breasts
- 6 slices Swiss cheese
- 6 slices good-quality ham
- 4 Tbsp. white flour
- Pinch cayenne pepper
- 8 Tbsp. butter
- ½ cup white wine
- 1 tsp. chicken bouillon granules
- 1 Tbsp. tapioca or cornstarch
- 1 cup whipping cream

Directions:

1. Use a mallet to pound the chicken breasts.
2. Top each chicken breast with 1 slice of ham and 1 slice of cheese.
3. Fold the chicken breasts over with the filling inside. Fasten the chicken with a tooth pick.
4. Combine the flour with the paprika in a shallow bowl.
5. Dredge the chicken breasts through the seasoned flour.
6. Melt the butter in a skillet and brown the chicken evenly.
7. Pour in the wine and chicken granules.
8. Simmer the chicken for about 30 minutes.
9. Arrange the chicken pieces on a platter.
10. Mix together the cream and the cornstarch.
11. Stir the cream into the skillet and stir to combine with the juices.
12. Drizzle the sauce over the chicken.
13. Serve with mashed potatoes.

Poulet Basquaise – Chicken and Tomato Casserole

Serves: 4

Cooking Time: 40 minutes

Poulet Basquaise is another great dish from France's Basque region, which has a Spanish influence. It's just a tad spicier than a lot of French cooking, and it is delicious.

Ingredients:

- 2 Tbsp. olive oil
- 4 chicken thighs with bones and skin
- 2 chopped small onions
- 2 minced garlic cloves
- 1/3 cup white wine
- 2 diced bell peppers (for more heat, you can add a bit of diced chili pepper)
- 2 diced tomatoes
- ¼ tsp. paprika
- ¼ tsp. thyme
- Salt and pepper to taste

Directions:

1. Heat the olive oil in a large skillet.
2. Brown the chicken thighs for 10 minutes on all sides.
3. Place the chicken on a plate and drain the fat from the skillet.
4. Place the garlic and onion in the same skillet and sauté for about 2 minutes.
5. Pour in the wine and deglaze the skillet using a wooden spoon.
6. Add the remaining ingredients and put the chicken back in the skillet.
7. Let the chicken simmer for 30 minutes. Check for doneness.
8. Serve this with rice.

Roasted Chicken with Garlic

Servings: 4

Cooking Time: 1 hour

French cooking usually depends on the proper spices, so don't let the 40 garlic cloves scare you. When cooked, they turn sweet and mild. It only comes to about 5 or 6 whole garlic cloves. This is a buttery roasted chicken done the French way.

Ingredients:

- 40 garlic cloves
- 1 4-lb. chicken
- 3 Tbsp. butter
- Salt and pepper to taste
- 6 sprigs of fresh thyme

Directions:

1. Preheat the oven to 475 degrees F.

2. Place the chicken in a roasting pan

3. Rub 1 Tbsp. of butter all over the chicken; lift the skin flaps to butter underneath.

4. Season the chicken with the salt and pepper

5. Place the garlic cloves, thyme and 2 Tbsp. of butter around the chicken.

6. Roast for approximately 1 hour. Keep basting the chicken and checking on doneness.
7. Let the roasted chicken rest on a platter for 15 minutes.
8. Carve and serve with the pan juices and the garlic.

Coq au Vin

Of course, the French will simmer their chicken in wine. Letting the chicken simmer makes it juicy as it absorbs the liquid. The pearl onions are elegant, making this the perfect company dinner.

Servings: 6

Cooking Time: 55 minutes

Ingredients:

- 4 cups red wine
- 1 sliced onion
- 1 bouquet garni (with thyme, bay leaves, and parsley)
- 3 Tbsp. olive oil
- 1 ½ cup pearl onions that have been peeled
- 1 ½ cup sliced mushrooms
- 10 oz. of chopped bacon
- 3 Tbsp. butter
- 3 lbs. chicken thighs
- 2 Tbsp. flour
- 1 cup chicken stock, preferably homemade
- Salt and pepper to taste

Directions:

1. Place the chicken thighs in a bowl and add the wine and bouquet garni.
2. Cover and refrigerate overnight.
3. Use tongs to place the chicken on a plate.
4. Strain the liquid until only the wine remains. Set aside the bouquet garni.
5. Heat the olive oil in a Dutch oven.
6. Sauté the pearl onions in it for 8 to 10 minutes.
7. Transfer the onions to a plate.
8. Sauté the mushrooms in the same Dutch oven for 8 to 10 minutes.
9. Transfer the mushrooms to the plate with the pearl onions.
10. Add the bacon pieces to the Dutch oven and stir for 10 minutes.
11. Drain the bacon on a paper towel.
12. Heat 1 Tbsp. of the butter and brown the chicken. Season with the salt and pepper.
13. Place the browned chicken on a plate.
14. Sauté the onions for 10 minutes.
15. Sprinkle the onions with the flour and stir for 2 minutes.
16. Pour in the wine and chicken stock and stir to combine with the onions.
17. Return the thighs and bouquet garni to the Dutch oven.
18. Bring the liquid to a boil.
19. Reduce the cooking temperature and cook the chicken for 15 minutes. Give the liquid an occasional stir.
20. Add in the mushrooms.
21. Serve the chicken topped with the bacon pieces and some parsley over noodles.

Duck Recipes

Duck Cassoulet

Cassoulet is a complex French stew made with beans that originated in the southern French province of Languedoc. Blame England's Black Prince- when the legendary British prince tried to attack Languedoc, its unhappy and hungry citizens took their food supply and prepared a stew in a huge cauldron to ward off famine. They must have had lots of beans. Cassoulet can be made with a variety of meat, but duck or goose are traditional. This particular version, made with duck, is deliciously rich. Simmering the meat and beans allows for the flavors to really meld.

Servings: 10

Cooking Times: 9 hours and 30 minutes

Ingredients:

- 1 lb. sliced pork sausage
- ¾ Tbsp. whole cloves
- 1 onion, uncut
- 3 parsley sprigs
- 1/2 lb. slab bacon
- 1 rosemary sprig
- 1 lb. navy beans left to soak in water overnight
- 1 bay leaf
- 4 sliced carrots

- 3 minced garlic cloves
- 1 lb. duck breast cut into strips.
- 1 chopped tomato

Directions:

1. Brown the pork sausage in a skillet.
2. Press the cloves into the whole onion.
3. Tie the herbs in a cheese cloth (bouquet garni).
4. Place the beans (which have been soaked overnight), bacon, browned sausage, onion, garlic, carrots, bouquet garni, and duck slices in a large pot.
5. Cover the ingredients with water.
6. Cook on high heat for an hour, then lower the heat to a simmer and cook for another 8 hours.
7. Discard the slab bacon, bouquet garni and onion.
8. Add the tomato and stir.
9. Let cook for half an hour longer and serve.

Canard a l'Orange (Duck with Orange Sauce)

This dish is French cooking royalty. And it is definitely fit a king. Fussy Sun King Louis XIV had Duck à l'Orange added to his cookbook. It's hard to resist that crispy skin, savory meat, and sunshiny sauce. It's as French as the Marseillaise. Serve it with a helping of wild rice.

Serves: 8

Cooking Time: 3 hours

Ingredients:

- 2 5-lb. ducks
- Salt and pepper to taste
- 1 cup water
- Ingredients for Orange Sauce
- 1 tablespoon vegetable oil
- ¾ cups each chopped carrots, leeks, onions.
- ½ cup each chopped tomatoes and celery
- 2 bay leaves
- 2 crushed garlic cloves
- 2 Tbsp. tomato paste
- 1 tsp. thyme

- 3 Tbsp. white flour
- 4 cups chicken stock, preferably homemade
- 1 cup white wine
- 5 oranges
- 1/3 cup sugar
- 1/3 cup apple cider vinegar
- Salt and pepper to taste
- 2 -3 Tbsp. Grand Marnier
- 2 Tbsp. butter

Directions:

1. Preheat the oven to 425 degrees F.
2. Remove the gizzards and the wings from the ducks and keep separate.
3. Salt and pepper the ducks, inside and outside.
4. Place the ducks on a roasting rack, breast side up.
5. Add a cup of water and roast the ducks for 1 hour.
6. Discard all of the accumulated fat, then roast the ducks for 45 more minutes.
7. Prepare the sauce while the ducks roast.
8. Chop the gizzards and cut the wings in half.
9. Use a large pot to sauté the gizzards and wings in the vegetable oil for 20 minutes.
10. Put in the herbs, garlic, and vegetables, and cook for another 5 minutes.
11. Add the flour and tomato paste and stir thoroughly.
12. Pour in the wine and chicken stock and let the liquid boil.
13. Reduce the heat and simmer for about 1 hour.
14. Use a sieve to strain out the sauce. There should be about 3 cups of liquid.
15. Zest one orange and blanch the zest in boiling water. Strain the orange zest and set aside.
16. Juice the zested orange and a second orange to get 1 cup of orange juice.
17. Peel the last 3 oranges and remove the membranes from the sections. Set aside.

18. Transfer the roasted ducks to an ovenproof dish. Keep them warm.

19. Skim as much fat as possible from the juices left in the roasting pan. Add the orange sauce and roasting juices to a pan and bring to a boil. Strain the sauce.

20. In another pan, stir together the vinegar and sugar and let come to a boil for 3 – 4 minutes.

21. Stir in the orange juice and jelly and let the liquid boil again.

22. Stir in the sauce and let simmer 8 – 10 minutes.

23. Adjust the seasoning and add the Grand Marnier.

24. Stir in the butter and let it melt into the sauce.

25. Drizzle the ducks with the orange sauce and garnish with the orange zest.

26. Serve the ducks with the sauce.

(Canard aux Framboises) Duck Breasts with Raspberry Sauce

It's a shame Americans don't eat more rich duck meat the way the French do. Maybe it's the rendering of duck fat that deters many cooks. The French save the tasty duck fat for future cooking and sautéing. It's actually healthier than butter. Duck with liqueur-based fruit sauces is a perfect marriage, and we should savor more of it. Use frozen raspberries for this recipe if fresh ones aren't available.

Serves: 2

Cooking Time: 30 minutes

Ingredients:

- 2 halved duck breasts
- 2 tsp. salt
- 2 tsp. cinnamon
- 2 Tbsp. sugar
- 1/2 cup red wine
- ¼ cup creme de cassis
- 1 tsp. cornstarch
- ¼ lb. raspberries

Directions:

1. Preheat the broiler.
2. With a fork, stab through the fat and skin of the breasts.
3. Get a skillet hot and fry the breasts with the skin down. The skin should be brown and draining of fat within approximately 10 minutes.
4. Discard most of the fat and continue frying for 10 more minutes.
5. Transfer the duck breasts to a baking sheet.
6. In a bowl, mix together the sugar, salt, and cinnamon.
7. Drizzle the mixture over the duck breasts
8. Discard the fat remaining in the skillet.
9. Combine the liqueur, wine, and cornstarch, and stir.
10. Pour the liquid into the skillet and let simmer for a few minutes. Keep stirring as the liquid thickens.
11. Stir in the raspberries while continuing to simmer for another minute.
12. Place the duck under the broiler for 1 minute. The sugar should caramelize.
13. Cut the duck into thin slices and top with the raspberry sauce.

Pork Recipes

Croque Madame and Croque Monsieur

Serves: 4

Cooking Time: 5-8 minutes

Croque Madame and Croque Monsieur are luncheon staples of French cooking. Legend has it that in 1901, a Parisian bistro ran out of baguettes. Quelle Horreur! The chef used a load of sandwich bread and filled it with ham and cheese and crisped it. The official version of this broiled sandwich is served with a béchamel sauce.

Croque Madame is the same sandwich served with a fried or poached egg on top. It's referred to as Croque Madame because the egg supposedly looks like a lady's hat. Croque Madame was created in 1960, when women and women's fashion were making a huge splash. (But who wants to wear a hat resembling an egg?)

Ingredients:

- ¼ cup of unsalted butter
- 2 Tbsp. flour
- 1 cup whole milk
- ¼ tsp. salt
- ¼ cup freshly grated Parmesan
- 8 slices sandwich bread or sourdough bread
- 12 slices of good ham such as Black Forest

- 12 oz. grated Gruyere or Swiss cheese
- 4 eggs

Directions:

1. Preheat the broiler.
2. Prepare the béchamel sauce by first melting 2 oz. of butter.
3. Stir in the flour and keep stirring for about 3 minutes. The butter shouldn't brown, just incorporate it with the flour.
4. Add the cup of milk. Stir a few times for about 10 minutes.
5. Add the Parmesan and let it melt.
6. Transfer the béchamel sauce to a bowl.
7. Stir half of the Gruyere or Swiss into the béchamel sauce.
8. Lay out 4 slices of the bread.
9. Cover each slice with the ham and spoon some sauce on top of the ham.
10. Melt half of the remaining butter in a skillet.
11. Brown 2 sandwiches for 2 minutes on each side.
12. Place the sandwiches on a baking sheet.
13. Repeat this with the remaining bread.
14. For the Croque Madame, coat the skillet with a nonstick spray. Fry up 2 eggs at a time.
15. Broil the sandwiches for about 2 minutes.
16. For the Croque Madame, top each sandwich with an egg.

Pork Aux Champignons (Pork and Mushrooms)

French cooking involves a lot of simmering to bring out the flavors. These pork chops simmer in a wonderful mushroom sauce.

Serves: 4

Cooking Time: 1 hour 10 minutes

Ingredients:

- 2 ½ lbs. of pork tenderloins
- 2 Tbsp. vegetable oil
- Salt and pepper to taste
- 1 lb. mushrooms
- 2 diced garlic cloves
- 1 bay leaf
- 2 whole cloves
- 2 medium shallots
- 8 pearl onions
- 1 sprig of thyme
- 1 cup heavy cream

Directions:

1. Cut the pork into round medallions that are an inch thick.
2. Heat the oil in a skill and brown the medallions.
3. Salt and pepper the meat to taste.
4. Slice the mushrooms.
5. Add the sliced mushrooms, cloves, bay leaf, and garlic to the pork.
6. Peel and slice the shallots and peel the pearl onions.
7. Add them to the skillet with the thyme.
8. Cover the skillet and cook on low heat for an hour.
9. Remove all the herbs.
10. Stir in the heavy cream.
11. Serve with some rice.

Pork in Port Wine

These pork medallions are quickly sautéed in a nice port. The sweetness of the port works well here. A great French meal for company or for a weekend. Serve the pork with roasted potatoes.

Servings: 2

Cooking Time: 5 minutes

Ingredients:

- ¾ lb. pork tenderloin
- 1 tsp. olive oil
- Salt and pepper to taste
- ¾ cup port
- ½ cup chicken stock
- 2 Tbsp. tomato sauce
- ½ tsp. oregano

Directions:

1. Cut the tenderloin into slices about 1 inch thick.

2. In a skillet, sauté the medallions in the heated oil for about 5 minutes, flipping sides while you're cooking.

3. Season the pork with salt and pepper.

4. Place the pork on 2 plates.

5. Pour the port wine in the skillet, letting it boil while you scrape up the bottom of the pan. After a minute, stir in the chicken stock and tomato sauce. Add the thyme.

6. Drizzle the sauce over the pork.

Lamb Recipes

Lamb Navarin

Lamb is a very versatile animal. It gives us both food, milk, and clothing. Braising started in France in the 19th century as a means of tenderizing inferior pieces of meat. Letting the lamb braise makes it tender and helps retain its juices. Lamb Navarin is another country stew elevated to cuisine. It is named after the navet, which is French for turnip and an important part of this dish. French cooking is invariably filled with fresh, seasonal vegetables.

Serves: 4

Cooking Time: 1 hours and 15 minutes

Ingredients:

- 2 Tbsp. olive oil
- 1 ½ lb. lamb shoulder meat, cut into bite-sized pieces
- Salt and pepper to taste
- 5 carrots cut into 2-inch chunks
- 1 chopped onion
- 2 crushed garlic cloves
- 2 Tbsp. flour
- 2 Tbsp. tomato paste
- 4 cups of white wine

- 4 turnips cut into 2-inch chunks
- 4 new potatoes cut into 2-inch chunks
- 4 Tbsp. butter
- 2 tsp. sugar
- 10 peeled pearl onions
- 1/3 cup frozen peas
- Garnish: chopped parsley

Directions:

1. Preheat the oven to 350 degrees F.
2. Use a Dutch oven and heat up the olive oil.
3. Salt and pepper the lamb and sauté the lamb on all sides.
4. Transfer the lamb to a platter.
5. Place the onion and 3 of the carrots in the Dutch oven and cook for 10 minutes, until they soften.
6. Add in the flour, tomato paste, and garlic and stir well for 2 minutes.
7. Pour in the wine and 1 cup of water and add the sautéed lamb.
8. Stir well and bring the liquid to a boil.
9. Place the Dutch oven into the preheated oven and cook for 50 minutes. The lamb should be tender.
10. Use a slotted spoon to place the lamb on a large platter and keep the meat warm.
11. Strain the cooking liquid into a medium saucepan.
12. Toss the solids.
13. Bring the liquid to a boil for 25 minutes. The liquid should be reduced to about 2 ½ cups. Set aside.
14. Place the potatoes in some water and set aside.
15. Heat a skillet and melt the butter. Add the remaining carrots, salt, sugar, and 1 cup of water. Partially cover the skillet and cook for 12 minutes.
16. Add in the pearl onions and turnip and cook until vegetables are done and tender.
17. The water should be evaporated. Stir the vegetables for a few minutes until they brown.

18. Set the vegetables aside and cover to keep warm.

19. Cook the potatoes until they are done. Place them on a platter and set aside.

20. Return the meat and vegetables to the sauce, and heat everything.

21. Garnish the stew with parsley.

Roast Leg of Lamb

Roast Lamb in a favorite French Easter tradition. Roast the potatoes with the lamb for extra yumminess. This recipe has only a few ingredients, and the easy seasoning lets the lamb flavor shine through. Serve with some fresh springtime asparagus.

Serves: 6

Cooking Time: 1 hour 45 minutes

Ingredients:

- 1 5-lb leg of lamb
- 4 sliced garlic cloves
- 2 Tbsp. rosemary
- Salt and pepper to taste

Directions:

1. Preheat the oven to 350 degrees F.
2. Use a sharp knife to cut slits into the top of the lamb.
3. Insert a slice of garlic into each slit.
4. Season with salt and pepper.
5. Place the rosemary on the bottom of a roasting pan and top with the leg of

lamb.

6. Roast for 1 ¾ hours to 2 hours. Lamb does not need to be fully cooked through.

7. Let the lamb sit for a few minutes, then carve into slices.

Gigot a La Cuillère (Slow Simmered Lamb)

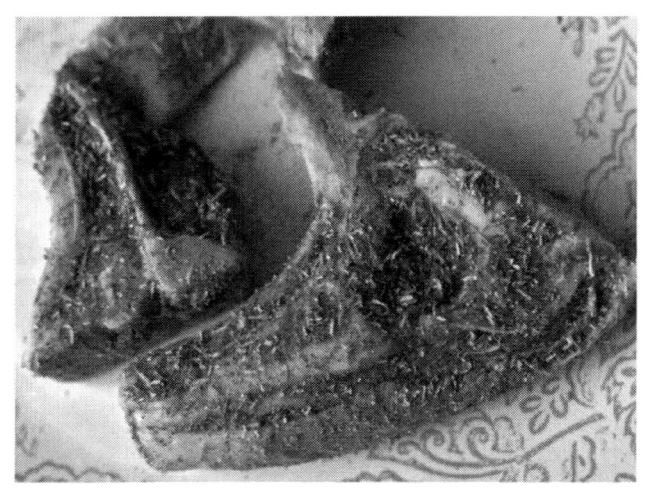

Lamb slow-cooked in wine and cognac is a French tradition. The meat is fall-off-the-bones tender, and traditionally, it is carved with a spoon.

Serves: 6 - 8

Cooking Time: 7 hours and 30 minutes

Ingredients:

- 1 leg of lamb
- 4 sliced onions
- 10 whole cloves of garlic
- 4 sliced carrots
- ¼ cup white wine
- 1 ¼ cup stock (beef or lamb)
- 3 Tbsp. cognac
- Salt and pepper to taste

Directions

1. Preheat the oven to 250 degrees F. The roast will be simmering low and slowly.
2. Brown all sides of the lamb in a skillet.
3. Place the lamb and the vegetables in a Dutch oven.

4. Pour in the stock and white wine, and stir in the seasoning.
5. Cover the Dutch oven with a lid and cook for 7 hours.
6. Place the lamb and vegetables on a platter.
7. Transfer the cooking juices to a saucepan and skim off the fat.
8. Bring the liquid to a boil and reduce it by about a quarter.
9. Stir in the cognac.
10. Carve the lamb – with a spoon, if you wish – and serve with the sauce.

Seafood Recipes

Trout Meunière Amandine (Trout with Brown Butter Sauce and Almonds)

France is a virtual paradise for those who fish. In the clear streams of the Pyrénées, fresh trout line up to be caught. A brown butter sauce is a popular French accompaniment for fish. This recipe adds a few almonds for extra pizzazz.

Serves: 4

Cooking Time: 5 minutes

Ingredients:

- 1 cup unsalted butter
- 1 Tbsp. apple cider vinegar
- 2 tsp. lemon juice
- 1 Tbsp. vegetable oil
- 2 cups whole milk
- 2 large eggs
- 2 cups white flour
- 4 deboned trout fillets
- Salt and pepper to taste

- 3 cups toasted sliced almonds

Directions:

1. To make the sauce, melt the butter in a skillet over low heat for about 20 minutes. Stir occasionally. Remove the melted butter from the stove and stir in the lemon juice and apple cider vinegar. Whisk vigorously and set aside.

2. Heat the oil in another skillet until it is very hot.

3. Lay out two shallow plates. Fill one with the flour. In the other, whisk together the eggs and milk.

4. Salt and pepper the trout.

5. Dip one fillet in the flour first, then the eggs. Then dip it in the flour a second time.

6. Place the fillet on a rack placed in a baking dish.

7. Repeat this with the remaining fillets.

8. Fry the trout for about 5 minutes. Drain the fillets on a paper towel.

9. Place each fillet on a plate and top with some almonds.

10. Spoon brown butter sauce over each fillet.

Moules à la Marinière

The French area of Brittany is famed for its specially cultivated mussels. To prepare them à la marinière, braise the mussels in some white wine. The French hold a large empty shell between thumb and forefinger to pull out the luscious mussel meat from the other mussel shells. Before preparing the mussels, be sure to wash them thoroughly.

Serves: 4 – 6

Cooking Time: 5 minutes

Ingredients:

- 2 cups of dry white wine
- ¼ cup diced scallions
- 6 sprigs of parsley
- ¼ tsp. thyme
- Dash of pepper
- 6 Tbsp. butter
- 2 lbs. mussels
- ¾ cup chopped parsley

Directions:

1. Place all of the ingredients except for the mussels and chopped parsley in a large pot.

2. Let the liquid boil for about 3 minutes to allow the alcohol to evaporate.

3. Toss in the mussels and cover the pot. Bring the liquid to a boil again.

4. Let the mussels boil for 5 minutes, until the shells have opened. Discard any unopened shells.

5. Ladle the mussels into plates.

6. Cover the mussels with the cooking broth and top with parsley.

7. The broth tastes heavenly, so have enough French bread handy to soak it up.

Salmon Crepes

Crepes aren't just for breakfast. Fill a crepe with savory seafood, and you have a very satisfying meal. For extra ease, the fish and the sauce are cooked simultaneously. The French would serve this with a small salad or a baguette on the side.

Serves: 6

Cooking Times: 30

Ingredients:

- 12 crepes (see breakfast crepe recipe)
- 1 lb. salmon filets
- 1 chopped leek
- 4 Tbsp. butter
- 3 Tbsp. flour
- ¼ cup white wine
- 1 ½ cups milk
- ½ cup grated Swiss cheese
- Dash of nutmeg
- Salt and pepper to taste

Directions:

1. Prepare the crepes first and set aside.
2. Wash the leeks thoroughly, then sauté them in the butter for 3 minutes.
3. Place the fillets in the skillet with the leeks and cook for a few minutes. Flake the fish into small chunks.
4. When the fish is cooked through, sprinkle the flour over it and stir to mix thoroughly.
5. Add the milk and wine and stir. Let the liquid boil while stirring.
6. Remove the skillet from the heat and add in half of the Swiss cheese. Stir as it melts.
7. Season with the nutmeg, salt, and pepper.
8. Spoon the salmon filling into the center of each crepe.
9. Flip one end of the crepe over the other to close it.
10. Lightly butter a baking sheet.
11. Arrange the crepes on the baking sheet and top with the rest of the Swiss cheese.
12. Bake for 20 minutes at 350 degrees F.

Cognac Shrimp

The sweetness of the caramelized shallots really make this dish. As is customary in French cooking, the creamy sauce is made with alcohol, this time a nice cognac. Serve the shrimp with pasta or a crusty French bread.

Serves: 4

Cooking Times: 10 minutes

Ingredients:

- 2 Tbsp. olive oil
- 2 minced garlic cloves
- 6 Tbsp. minced shallots
- 1 lb. shelled and deveined shrimp
- Salt and pepper to taste
- ¼ cup sliced sun-dried tomatoes packed in oil
- ½ cup cognac
- ½ cup half-and-half

Directions:

1. Heat the olive oil and sauté the shallots and garlic until they become fragrant.
2. Add the shrimp, sun-dried tomatoes, salt, and pepper. Stir well.
3. Cook the shrimp for 5 minutes.
4. Pour in the cognac and deglaze the pan with a wooden spoon.

5. Cook for 5 minutes. The sauce should be a bit thick.

Bouillabaisse

It is impossible to discuss French cooking with mentioning Bouillabaisse. When hungry fishermen in Marseille returned from the sea, they wanted to fix a meal. Rather than wasting their expensive catch of the day, they used common cheap fish that they couldn't sell. They boiled the fish in water with fennel and garlic. By the 17th century, when tomatoes were introduced to France, they were added. Marseille became a prosperous trading city in the 19th century, with fancy hotels and restaurants. Bouillabaisse was slowly refined for upper class visitors, using fish stock instead of water and adding saffron. This dish uses fresh local seafood, which will differ according to the season. The seafood in this recipe are suggestions. The important thing is that the fish and shellfish are absolutely fresh and that it is not overcooked. Bouillabaisse is served with a garlic sauce called rouille, which is the dish's crowning touch. This dish takes a bit of effort, but the gasps of and pleasure and awe from your guests makes it worth it.

Serves: 8

Cooking Time: 1 hour 5 minutes

Ingredients for the Rouille:

- One 3-inch pieces of baguette, cut into 1/2-inch rounds
- 2 garlic cloves (1 for the rouille and 1 to rub on the bread)

- 3 Tbsp. water
- 1/2 teaspoon of kosher salt
- 1/2 teaspoon of cayenne pepper
- 3 Tbsp. of extra-virgin olive oil

Ingredients for the Bouillabaisse:
- 3 Tbsp. good-quality olive oil
- 2 sliced leeks
- 1 sliced onion
- 1 cut up fennel bulb—keep the fronds in reserve
- 4 chopped garlic cloves
- 2 diced tomatoes
- 2 bay leaves
- 1/8 tsp. saffron threads
- 2 Tbsp. Pernod or ouzo
- 5 cups fish stock – either store-bought or homemade
- 1 live lobster
- 8 baguette slices
- 1 ½ lb. cubed potatoes
- 24 littleneck clams
- 1 lb. halibut or mahi-mahi, cut to bite sized pieces
- 1 lb. flounder or red sea bass, cut to bite sized pieces
- 1 lb. sole or striped bass, cut to bite sized pieces

Directions:

1. To make the rouille, sprinkle a few drops of water on the bread and let side for 5 minutes.

2. Place the bread in the food processor and add the remaining ingredients except the oil.

3. Chop the bread until it has a coarse texture.

4. Slowly drizzle in the oil and process the rouille until it is smooth.

5. Refrigerate the rouille.

6. Warm the olive oil in a skillet and sauté the fennel, onion, garlic and leeks

for 5 minutes.

7. Stir in the tomatoes and let cook for another 5 minutes.

8. Put the saffron, bay leaves, and Pernod in the skillet and stir.

9. Pour in the fish stock and let simmer for 20 minutes. The vegetables should be done.

10. Toss out the bay leaves.

11. Transfer the broth to a food processor and puree.

12. Strain the puree into the skillet.

13. Fill a large pot with water and bring to boil.

14. Cook the lobster for 4 minutes. Use cold water to rinse and cool it.

15. Remove all of the outer shells and cut the lobster meat into bite-sized chunks.

16. Preheat the broiler. Place the bread slices on a baking pan and broil for 5 minutes.

17. Rub the bread with the garlic and lightly cover it with olive oil.

18. Return the broth to the pot.

19. Stir in the cayenne pepper and potato chunks and stir.

20. Let simmer for 15 minutes, until the potatoes are done.

21. Season with salt and pepper.

22. Add the clams and cook for 4 minutes, until they open.

23. Add all remaining seafood and cover.

24. Simmer for 5- 8 minutes.

25. Divide the toast into the 8 bowls.

26. Fill the bowl with the stew and top with the rouille.

27. Garnish with some fennel fronds.

Lighter French Fare (Soup and Salads)

Asparagus and Ham with Poached Egg

This salad is a favorite French bistro lunch. Fresh asparagus and greens topped with a poached egg are irresistible.

Serves: 4

Cooking Time: 8 minutes

Ingredients:

- 3 Tbsp. salt
- 1 lb. trimmed asparagus spears
- 4 large eggs
- 1 Tbsp. cider vinegar
- 4 cups chopped greens
- ¼ cup chopped chives
- Vinaigrette (see below)
- 4 slices good-quality ham
- Salt and pepper for pepper
- Toast

Directions:

1. Fill a bowl with ice water.

2. Cook the asparagus in a pot of boiling water until tender.

3. Place the cooked asparagus in a colander and put into the ice water to blanche them. This will keep them nice and crisp.

4. Drain the asparagus in a paper or cloth towel and put them on a plate.

5. Line up 4 ramekins and break an egg into each one.

6. In a saucepan, boil 1 – 2 inches of water and the vinegar.

7. Use the ramekins to gently slip each egg into the boiling water.

8. Cover the saucepan and let the eggs poach with the heat turned off.

9. In 3 minutes, the egg white should be firm, while the yolks are soft.

10. Use a slotted spoon to move the eggs to a plate.

11. Toss the greens and chives in a salad bowl with the vinaigrette.

12. To arrange the salad on a plate, put the greens on one side and place a poached egg next or almost on top of it. Four asparagus go alongside the egg. Cover each egg with a ham slice.

13. Season with salt and pepper to taste and add the chives.

14. If desired, serve the salad with toast.

Ingredients for Vinaigrette:
- ¼ cup good-quality olive oil
- ¼ tsp salt
- 1 Tbsp. lemon juice

Directions:

1. Combine all of the ingredients and mix thoroughly. Placing them in a jar and shaking the jar vigorously works well.

Macaroni Beaucaire

This French comfort food comes from the Provence town of Beaucaire. Pasta and cheese are incorporated with fresh tomatoes and healthful eggplants.

Serves: 6

Cooking Time: 30 minutes

Ingredients for the Pasta:

- 1 cup elbow macaroni
- ¼ cup olive oil
- 3 Tbsp. grated gruyere cheese
- Salt and pepper to taste
- ¼ cup chopped chives

Ingredients for the Vegetables:

- ½ cup vegetable oil
- 2 eggplants – cut into ½" slices
- Salt to taste
- 3 tomatoes – cut into thin slices
- 1 cup shredded sharp cheddar cheese

Directions:

1. Cook the macaroni in salt water until the noodles are just done.
2. Ladle half a cup of the cooking liquid into a bowl.
3. Drain the remaining liquid.
4. To the reserved cooking liquid, mix in the gruyere cheese, olive oil, salt, and pepper.
5. Mix well to melt the cheese.
6. Add in the macaroni and chives, mix, and set aside.
7. Bring 2 Tbsp. of vegetable oil to a high heat in a skillet.
8. Make a layer of eggplant slices in the skillet and season with salt.
9. Cook the eggplant slices for 3 minutes on both sides.
10. Use a slotted spoon to remove the slices from the skillet and repeat until all of the eggplant slices have been browned. Add additional oil if necessary
11. Preheat the oven to 400 degrees F.
12. Keep 6 eggplant slices and 6 tomato slices reserved on a plate.
13. Arrange the remaining eggplant and tomatoes in a baking dish.
14. Cover the vegetables with the macaroni.
15. Cover the macaroni with the reserved slices of eggplant and tomato. Arrange them in an attractive pattern.
16. Top with the shredded cheddar cheese.
17. Bake for 20 minutes.

Salade au Chèvre Chaud (Goat Cheese Salad)

France is famous for its goat cheese. This classic French salad relies on simple ingredients for its flavors

Serves: 4

Cooking Times: 4 minutes

Ingredients for the Cheese Toasts:
- 4 baguette slices
- 4 thick slices of goat cheese
- 1 tsp. olive oil

Ingredients for the Salad:
- 6 oz. of any greens – spinach, baby greens or arugula
- 4 Tbsp. good-quality olive oil
- 4 Tbsp. white wine vinegar
- 1 tsp. honey
- Salt and pepper to taste

Directions:

1. Preheat the oven to 475 degrees F.
2. Arrange the baguette slices on a cooking sheet.

3. Top each slice of bread with a slice of goat cheese.

4. Drizzle the cheese with olive oil.

5. Bake the baguettes for about 5 minutes. Keep an eye on the bread to prevent it from burning. Remove the bread from oven and allow to cool.

6. Wash the greens under running water.

7. Mix together all of the vinaigrette ingredients and drizzle over the greens.

8. Divide the greens onto 4 plates and top with the toast. Serve while still hot.

Salad Niçoise

This 19th century classic French salad usually includes tuna and anchovies, green beans, tomatoes, and, of course, boiled eggs. You can add other favorites, such as peppers, artichokes or onions. What matters is the presentation. The contrast of colors, shapes and texture are an important ingredient. Salad Niçoise is all about looking elegant. Use tuna packed in oil, and drizzle the salad with the accompanying vinaigrette.

Salad Niçoise was created in the city of Nice, and even today, they are traditionalists, arguing about whether boiled vegetables or only raw ones should be included. While they argue, prepare the salad and enjoy.

Serving: 4

Cooking Times: 15 minutes

Ingredients for the Vinaigrette:

- ¾ cup olive oil
- ¼ cup lemon juice
- ¼ cup champagne vinegar
- 2 ½ tsp. Dijon mustard
- 1 smashed garlic clove
- 1/8 tsp. lemon zest
- Salt and pepper to taste
- Ingredients for the Salad:

- 1 lb. small yellow potatoes
- 1 cup green beans
- 4 Tbsp. softened butter
- 3 cans of tuna in oil
- 4 sliced hard-boiled eggs
- 2 quartered tomatoes
- ½ cup Niçoise olives
- 3 cups greens

Directions for the Vinaigrette:

1. Blend the vinegar, oil, mustard, and garlic in a food processor until the ingredients are creamy.
2. Add the lemon zest and salt and pepper.
3. Blend well.

Directions for the Salad:

1. Boil the potatoes in salt water until they are done.
2. Place the potatoes in a bowl and set aside and let cool.
3. Boil more water and cook the green beans for 4 minutes, until they are done but still crispy. Set the green beans aside and let cool.
4. Slice the potatoes and drizzle with half the butter, salt and pepper.
5. Using another bowl, drizzle the green beans with the rest of the butter, salt and pepper.
6. In a third bowl, crumble the tuna and toss with 2 tablespoons of the vinaigrette, salt and pepper.
7. Arrange the greens on a platter. Place the green beans, sliced eggs, potatoes, olives and tuna on top of the greens.
8. Serve with the vinaigrette.

Onion Tart

This classic French tart makes the perfect light meal. The caramelized onions and Gruyère cheese melt together perfectly. Using a store-bough crust makes this recipe a snap to prepare. For a bit of extra kick, spread a bit of Dijon mustard on the bottom of the shell.

Serves: 6 - 8

Cooking Time: 1 hour 15 minutes

Ingredients:

- 2 Tbsp. olive oil
- 2 Tbsp. butter
- 4 thinly sliced onions
- Dash of sugar
- Salt and pepper to taste
- 3 eggs
- 1 1/3 cup whipping cream
- 1 ¼ oz. grated Gruyère cheese
- 1 partially baked pie shell

Directions:

1. Heat the olive oil and the butter in a skillet.

2. Add the onions and stir in the salt, pepper and sugar.

3. Sauté on very low head for about 30 minutes, until the onions are brown and caramelized.

4. Heat the oven to 375 degrees F.

5. Whisk together the whipping cream and eggs in a bowl.

6. Add the nutmeg, salt, and pepper.

7. Stir together the onions and the eggs. Add half the grated Gruyère. Stir thoroughly.

8. Distribute the filling into the pie shell and add the remaining Gruyère.

9. Bake the tart for about 45 minutes.

10. Let the tart cool before serving.

(Tartiflette) (Bacon, Potato, and Reblochon Casserole)

A rich casserole from the Savoy region gets its unique flavor from the Reblochon cheese, which has a very silky texture. If you can't find any Reblochon, try a good Fontina.

Serves: 6

Cooking Time: 50 minutes

Ingredients:

- 3 Tbsp. butter
- 8 oz. slab bacon chopped into 1 x ½-inch pieces
- 1 sliced onion
- ½ cup white wine
- 2 ½ sliced Russet potatoes
- Salt and pepper to taste
- 1 lb. reblochon cheese very thickly sliced

Directions:

1. Heat the oven to 375 degrees F.
2. Lightly butter a baking dish.
3. Fry the bacon in a skillet until it is crisp.
4. Use a slotted spoon to place the bacon on a plate with a paper towel to drain the fat.
5. Sauté the onion in the same skillet for 10 minutes.

6. Stir in the wine and bring the liquid to a boil.
7. Cook for 3 – 5 minutes.
8. Season the sliced potatoes with salt and pepper and add them to the skillet.
9. Cook until the potatoes are tender, about 10 minutes.
10. Cover the bottom of the baking dish with half of the potato mixture.
11. Top the potatoes with half of the bacon and half of the cheese.
12. Repeat the layering.
13. Bake the casserole for 25 minutes.

Soupe a l'oignon (French Onion Soup)

Onion soup is as old as the Romans. It was considered appropriate food for the poor, since onions are plentiful and cheap. In the 18th century Paris, French onion soup was elevated to bistro food with the luscious addition of cheese and croutons. In Roman times, onions were thought to be an aphrodisiac. In France's early days, newlyweds were given onion soup to recover from the exhausting wedding night.

Serves: 6

Cooking Time: 2 hours 35 minutes

Ingredients:

- 5 Tbsp. butter
- 2 ½ lbs. very thin onion slices
- ¼ tsp. salt
- ¼ tsp. sugar
- 1 Tbsp. flour
- 8 cups beef stock, preferably homemade
- ¼ cup brandy or cognac
- 1 cup white wine
- 8 thick toasted French bread slices
- 2 cups grated Gruyere cheese

Directions:

1. Heat 2 cups of beef stock.
2. Heat the butter in a large skillet or pot.
3. Sauté the onion slices until they are translucent.
4. Stir in the sugar and salt and let the onions caramelize for about 25 minutes. They should be a dark brown color.
5. Dust the onions with the flour and stir for 4 minutes.
6. Remove the pot from the heat and add in the 2 cups of heated stock. Blend well.
7. Adjust the stove temperature to simmer and add the remaining beef stock, wine, and cognac.
8. Cover the pot and simmer for 2 hours. If necessary, add some water.
9. Taste the soup and adjust the seasoning.
10. Distribute the soup among 4 heatproof bowls.
11. Place the toasted French bread on top and add the Gruyere cheese.
12. Line up the bowls on a baking sheet and place under broiler.
13. Broil for 2 – 3 minutes, until the cheese starts to turn crusty.
14. Serve immediately.

Potage Parmentier (Potato and Leek Soup)

Potage Parmentier is another brainchild of Antoine Parmentier, the French pharmacist who spent his life trying to get the French to eat potatoes. He succeeded admirably, and even King Louis XIV became a fan. Today, Parmentier has dishes named after him, and statues have been erected in his honor. Long live the potato!

Creamy and luscious potato and leek soup is easy to prepare. If you prefer a cold soup, simply let the Potage Parmentier chill, add some cream, and call it Vichyssoise! How very French of you.

Serves: 6

Cooking Time: 30 minutes

Ingredients:

- 1 lb. peeled and cubed Russet potatoes (Please do not use any other kind of potato.)
- 3 cups sliced leeks
- 6 cups chicken stock
- 1 Tbsp. salt
- 2 -3 tablespoons minced chives
- 2 bay leaves
- 1/8 tsp. thyme

Directions:

1. Cook the potatoes and leeks in the chicken stock until they are tender.
2. Puree the soup with a blender
3. Add the cream, salt, bay leaves, and thyme and simmer in a pot for about 15 minutes.
4. Remove the bay leaves.
5. Ladle soup into individual bowls and garnish with the chives.

Cauliflower and Cheese Soufflé

This delicious soufflé is a main meal when you add a salad. Enjoy.

Serves: 4

Cooking Time: 30 minutes

Ingredients:

- 3 Tbsp. grated parmesan cheese
- 1 cup chopped cauliflower florets
- Salt and pepper to taste
- 5 oz. goat cheese
- 1/8 tsp. nutmeg
- 3 large eggs
- 5 egg whites

Directions:

1. Heat the oven to 375 degrees F.
2. Lightly grease 4 ramekins and dust with the parmesan cheese.
3. Transfer the ramekins to a baking sheet.
4. Cook the cauliflower florets in boiling water.

5. Place the drained florets in a food processor with the eggs, goat cheese, nutmeg, salt, and pepper.
6. Puree the ingredients until they are smooth.
7. Place the pureed cauliflower in a bowl.
8. In another bowl, beat the egg white to a froth.
9. Fold the egg whites into the puree.
10. Divide the puree into the ramekins.
11. Bake for 30 minutes.
12. Serve with a salad.

Ratatouille

Ratatouille is the perfect showcase for fresh vegetables. This vegetarian stew from Provence works well in the summertime, when produce is at its freshest. This is another dish that negates the myth that French cooking is snobbish- this stew was put together by poor farmers as an inexpensive meal. The fact that it's delicious is just a bonus. It's usually made with zucchini, onions, eggplant, and green peppers, but you can use what you really like. Ratatouille can be eaten either hot or cold. For fun, add tomato sauce for a delicious pasta topping, or use it as a wonderful sandwich filling. When preparing, slice all of the vegetables very thin.

Servings: 6 - 8

Cooking Time: 45 minutes

Ingredients:

- 6 oz. tomato paste
- 1/2 onion, chopped
- 4 Tbsp. minced garlic clove
- 1 cup water
- Salt and pepper to taste
- 1 each, peeled and sliced: eggplant, zucchini, red and green bell pepper, yellow squash
- 2 Tbsp. olive oil

- 1 tsp. crushed thyme
- 4 Tbsp. mascarpone cheese

Directions:

1. Preheat the oven to 375 degrees F.
2. Cover the bottom of a baking dish with the tomato paste.
3. Add the garlic and onion.
4. Place the vegetable slices into the dish, alternating between different kinds. This is a chance to use colors.
5. Drizzle the olive oil over the dish and season with the salt, pepper, and thyme.
6. Cover the baking dish with aluminum foil.
7. Bake for 45 minutes. The vegetables should be very tender.
8. Top the ratatouille with the mascarpone cheese and serve.

Pan Bagnat

The pan bagnat is a specialty sandwich from France's Provence area. It's a sandwich that combines the fresh ingredients of a Salade Niçoise or a ratatouille, and adds some tuna or anchovies, (but never any mayonnaise). The longer this sandwich sits, the better the flavors will blend. It's a make-ahead sandwich bursting with flavor. If your friends aren't into French food, just tell them it's tuna sandwich. Then, maybe meet new people?

Servings: 6

Cooking Time: 0

Ingredients:

- 2 diced anchovy fillets
- 1 minced garlic clove
- 1 tsp. cider vinegar
- ½ tsp. Dijon mustard
- Salt and pepper to taste
- 1 Tbsp. olive oil
- 1 baguette cut in half
- 1 small sliced cucumber
- 1 sliced tomato
- 1 sliced small onion

- 1 can tuna fish in oil
- 6 basil leaves
- 2 Tbsp. sliced black olives
- 1 sliced boiled egg

Directions:

1. In a bowl, whisk together the anchovies, vinegar, garlic, mustard, salt, and pepper.
2. Slowly, add the oil while continuing to whisk.
3. Toss half of the cucumbers in the vinaigrette.
4. Place the other half the cucumbers slices on the bottom of a baguette half.
5. Top with onion slices, tomatoes, tuna, egg slices, olives, and basil.
6. Top the cucumbers with the vinaigrette.
7. Cover with second baguette half.
8. Wrap the sandwich in plastic.
9. Put a heavy weight, like a frying pan, on top of the sandwich for 8 -10 minutes.
10. Keep the sandwich unwrapped for 8 hours or slice immediately.

Desserts

Chocolate Banana Crepes

These crepes could very well be an excuse for the French to have chocolate for breakfast. And why not? They are sinfully delicious, but you can remind yourself just how healthful the banana is.

Serves: 4

Cooking Time: 25 minutes

Ingredients:

- 1 ½ cup milk
- 1 cup flour
- 2 Tbsp. sugar
- 1/8 tsp. salt
- 1 tsp. vanilla
- 3 large eggs
- ¼ cup melted butter
- 2 thinly sliced bananas
- ½ cup melted chocolate

Directions:

1. Combine the flour, milk, eggs, melted butter, vanilla, and salt in a blender.

Mix until you have a smooth batter.

2. Refrigerate the batter for an hour or overnight.

3. Lightly grease a skillet. Pour a third of a cup of batter into the skillet. Make sure the bottom of the skillet is covered.

4. Cook the crepe for about 3 minutes, flip it over with a plastic spatula, and cook the other side.

5. Cook for a minute or so until the crepe is nicely brown.

6. Continue to prepare all of the crepes. Add additional butter to the skillet if necessary.

7. Fold the crepes in half. Top with the sliced banana and melted chocolate.

Cappuccino Soufflé

Soufflés are considered a miracle of French cooking. A soufflé consists of a pudding base and egg whites. Soufflés are light and full of flavor. For dessert, they are sweet; if prepared for a main meal, they are made with savories such as cheese or crab.

Soufflés are intended to be impressive, which is why they are the perfect special after-dinner dessert.

Serve: 2

Cooking Time: 10

Ingredients:

- 1 tsp. butter
- 1 Tbsp. sugar
- ¼ cup sugar
- 1 Tbsp. instant coffee
- 2 tsp. vanilla
- Dash of cinnamon
- 2 egg whites
- Ingredients for Chocolate Sauce:
- ¼ cup of whipping cream
- 1 oz. semisweet chocolate

- 1 tsp. butter
- ¾ tsp. instant coffee

Directions:

1. Lightly butter 2 ramekins and dust the inside with sugar.

2. In a cup or bowl, mix together the instant coffee, cinnamon, and vanilla with a few drops of water.

3. Whip the egg whites and the cream of tartar with a hand beater.

4. Keep beating while adding ¼ cup sugar and the instant coffee.

5. Divide the mixture between the 2 ramekins.

6. Bake for 10 minutes. The soufflés should be puffy.

7. Combine all of the sauce ingredients and blend. You can melt the sauce in a microwave or in a small pan on the stove. Stir the sauce well.

8. Gently use a spoon to break the top of the soufflés and spoon in the sauce.

Pots de Créme

Pots de Créme is a custardy dessert that evolved in France during the 17th century. Chocolate was extremely expensive, and only the very rich were able to indulge. In the 16th century, fruit custards were popular. The chocolate custards prepared by royal French chefs for their wealthy patrons evolved from those fruit custards. It is rich in texture and flavor. While you can use store-bought whipped cream for this dessert, why would you? This dessert is worth preparing a batch of whipped cream at home.

Serves: 8

Cooking Time: 30 minutes

Ingredients:

- 1 ½ cups whipping cream
- ½ cup milk
- 4 oz. chopped bittersweet chocolate
- 1 oz. baker's chocolate
- 4 egg yolks
- 3 Tbsp. sugar
- Dash of salt
- Whipped cream

Directions:

1. Preheat the oven to 300 degrees F.

2. Combine the milk and heavy cream in a saucepan and bring to boil.

3. Remove the saucepan from the heat and stir in the chocolate pieces, stirring continuously until the mixture is creamy and smooth.

4. In another bowl, beat the egg yolks, salt, and sugar together.

5. Gently, let the hot chocolate mixture drizzle into the yolk mixture. Keep stirring.

6. Strain the mixture through a sieve into a bowl.

7. Distribute the mixture equally between the ramekins.

8. Arrange the ramekins in a casserole dish and place them in the oven.

9. Fill half of the dish with hot water.

10. Use aluminum foil to cover the ramekins. Prick a few holes along the length of the foil.

11. Bake the pot de cremes for 30 minutes. The edges should be firm and the center just a bit wiggly.

12. Refrigerate the ramekins for 3 hours.

13. Serve topped with whipped cream.

Crêpes Suzette

The Crepes Suzette is undoubtable the most famous of all the many French crepes. Like so much of French cooking, it depends on liqueur for its magnificence. Incredibly, this masterpiece was created from a mistake made by a 14 year-old assistant waiter named Henri Carpentier who was working in a Paris restaurant. Poor Henri was preparing dessert for the King Edward VII of England when he accidentally spilled some cordials into the chaffing dish. He set the future king's dish on fire! Edward was waiting, so the poor waiter had to serve him this flaming dish. One can imagine how horrified he was. But Edward love it and sipped the syrup with his spoon When Edward asked poor Henri the name of the dish, the waiter made up the name, Crepes Princesse. The lady who was dining with the future king asked whether he would name this delicious dish after her, Suzette. Thus a legend was born. I suspect Henri went on to a fine career.

Servings: 2

Cooking Time: 5 minutes

Ingredients for Crepes:

- 2 large eggs
- ¾ cup white flour
- ½ cup milk
- Dash of salt

- 1 tsp. sugar
- 1/3 cup cold water
- 1 Tbsp. olive oil
- 2 Tbsp. melted butter

Ingredients for the Orange Butter:
- 8 Tbsp. softened butter
- ¼ cup sugar
- 1 Tbsp. orange zest
- 1/3 cup orange juice
- ¼ cup Grand Marnier
- 2 Tbsp. cognac

Directions:
1. Whisk the flour, eggs, milk, sugar, and salt in a bowl.
2. Add in the olive oil, water, and butter.
3. Lightly grease a skillet.
4. Distribute 2 tablespoons of batter across the bottom of the skillet.
5. Cook on medium heat for about a minute. Turn the crepe and cook the other side for 10 - 15 seconds, until it just starts to brown.
6. Place the crepe on a platter or baking sheet and repeat with the remaining batter.
7. Place the butter, sugar, and orange zest in a food processor and process.
8. Preheat the broiler.
9. Butter a baking sheet and spirnkle it with sugar.
10. Fill the center of each crepe with 2 teaspoons of the orange mixture.
11. Fold the crepes over and arrange them on the baking sheet.
12. Dust the crepes with a bit of sugar, if you wish.
13. Broil the crepes for about 2 minutes.
14. Arrange the crepes on a platter.
15. Heat both spirits. Use a long match to ignite.
16. Spoon some of the liquid over the crepes and serve immediately.

Peach Melba

We can offer more thanks for Chef Escoffier for this creamy dessert. He prepared it especially for his friend, opera singer Nellie Melba, who often ate at his restaurant at the Savoy Hotel. The beauty of the dish lies in its simplicity - a ripe peach and vanilla ice cream with pureed raspberry.

Serves: 6

Cooking Time: 1 minute

Ingredients:

- 6 fresh peaches
- 2 Tbsp. sugar
- 2 cups vanilla ice cream
- 1 cup fresh raspberries
- 1 cup confectioner's sugar

Directions:

1. Bring a pot of water to boil. Lower the heat to a simmer, and place a peach in the water.
2. Simmer the peach for 15 seconds.
3. Use a slotted spoon to retrieve the peach and place it in ice water

immediately, then place the peach on a platter.

4. Repeat this with the rest of the peaches.
5. Peel the cooled peaches, cut them in half, and toss the pits.
6. Dust the peaches with sugar on all sides.
7. Return them to the platter and refrigerate for an hour.
8. Puree the raspberries in a food processor.
9. Strain the raspberry puree to get the liquid into a bowl.
10. Toss away the solids.
11. Stir the confectioner's sugar into the liquid and whisk vigorously to incorporate.
12. Let the raspberry syrup chill for at least an hour.
13. Line up 6 dessert dishes.
14. Fill each dish with a scoop of ice cream.
15. Top the ice cream with 2 of the peach halves.
16. Spoon the syrup over the peaches.

Baked Brie

Brie, of course, is the essential French cheese. You can bake it for a creamy, decadent dessert. Serve with crackers or slices of baguette.

Servings: 6 - 8
Cooking Times: 5 minutes
Ingredients:

- A wedge of Brie cheese
- ½ cup of chopped nuts, walnuts
- 2 Tbsp. honey
- ¼ tsp. cinnamon

Directions:

1. Preheat the oven to 350 degrees F.
2. Use a knife to cut the rind off the top of the Brie
3. Place the cheese on a baking dish
4. Brown the nuts in a skillet for a few minutes, then stir in the honey and cinnamon.
5. Spoon the nut syrup over the Brie.
6. Bake the Brie for 15 minutes.

Crème Brulee

Crème Brulee, made from egg yolks, is one of the smoothest of French desserts. The sugar crust adds a delightful crunch. This is sure to be a hit at any dinner gathering.

Servings: 6

Cooking Time: 15 minutes

Ingredients:

- 4 cups whipping cream
- 6 egg yolks
- 1 cup sugar
- 8 cups boiling water
- 1 vanilla bean

Directions:

1. Preheat the oven to 325 degrees F.
2. Open the vanilla bean and scrape out its contents into a saucepan.
3. Add the heavy cream and stir.
4. Bring the cream to a boil, then remove from the stove.
5. Cover the pan and let sit.

6. Discard the vanilla bean

7. In a bowl, whisk ½ cup sugar with the egg yolks. Blend them well.

8. Pour in the heavy cream very slowly while stirring.

9. Divide the liquid into 6 ramekins.

10. Line up the ramekins on a baking sheet.

11. Fill the bottom of the baking sheet with water so that the ramekins are covered halfway.

12. Bake the brulee for 45 minutes.

13. Refrigerate the ramekins with the brulee for 2 hours.

14. After removing the ramekins from the refrigerator, let sit for half an hour.

15. Sprinkle the remaining sugar on top of the 6 ramekins.

16. Carefully using a small torch, burn the sugar for 2 – 3 seconds until it melts.

Author's Afterthoughts

Thanks ever so much to each of my cherished readers for investing the time to read this book!

I know you could have picked from many other books but you chose this one. So a big thanks for buying this book and reading all the way to the end.

If you enjoyed this book or received value from it, I'd like to ask you for a favor.

Printed in Great Britain
by Amazon